Sally Ride

Written by Marcia S. Gresko
Illustrated by Wendy Chang

My name is Dan.
I am a reporter.
What's your name?

My name is Sally Ride.
I am an astronaut.
I was the first American
woman to travel in space.

Did you always want to be an astronaut?

No. When I was growing up, I liked to play baseball and tennis.

How did you become an astronaut?

I learned about space in school.
I went to astronaut school to learn to work in space.

What is it like in space?

In space, things float. Sometimes I ate sitting on the ceiling.

There are no beds.
You sleep in sleeping bags.
Your clothes have
lots of big pockets
to keep things in.

What jobs did you have in space?

I used the robot arm.

What will you remember most about your flight?

The thing I'll remember most is that it was fun.